ONE LESS ROAD TO TRAVEL

A COLLECTION OF POETRY

_9.26.98_

To Boo,

Enjoy !

Peace & Blessings,

Nichole L. Shields

by
NICHOLE L. SHIELDS

INTRODUCTION BY HAKI R. MADHUBUTI

First Printing

Library of Congress Catalog Card Number: 97-91342
ISBN: 0-9662036-0-7

Please contact Nichole L. Shields at
P.O. Box 4377
Chicago, IL 60680-4377
for permission to reproduce any parts of this book.

The award-winning poem *Momma in Red**
and *Southern Hospitality #2* have appeared
in Vol. 26 No. 2 of the Iowa Review.

This edition also includes the 1997
Gwendolyn Brooks Poetry Competition
award-winning poem *Southern Hospitality #4*.

Cover: Denise Borel; Layout: Paula LaPlace;
Editing/Proofreading: Okolo Ewunike
and Jawara James

*1995 Gwendolyn Brooks Poetry Competition

DEDICATION

This book is
dedicated to all of the e*ver*y day
down-to-earth people who inspire
me to write,

especially my Aunt Deloris Ivory;

two insightful friends,
Olivia Opirinade and Margaret Houston;

and to Lena Johnson,
a flower that had just begun to bloom.

They all have become ancestors and their
wisdom and memories will forever contribute to
my growth and development.

From the Author's Heart
♥ ♥ ♥ ♥ ♥ ♥ ♥ ♥ ♥ ♥ ♥ ♥ ♥ ♥

I would like to begin by giving praise to God for giving me the patience and endurance to remain on the straight and narrow path thus far in my life. We all know that while today may bring love and happiness, tomorrow may bring sorrow and pain, so again, I thank God. I would like to thank all that have made this book a reality, my mother, Barbara Turner, for never disregarding (as parents of artists often do) the many artistic ventures that I present to her, and for her everlasting love and support. I also thank my siblings (Chiquita, Quincy, and Eric) for their advice, wisdom, and support.

I can never thank Poet/Publisher/Educator Haki Madhubuti enough for giving The Writers Group his valuable time, wisdom, and honest critiques of our work at the Gwendolyn Brooks Center at Chicago State University. The wisdom shared with the group of writers has guided us in the write/right/write direction to produce good literature.

There are so many that have helped in the development of this book that I would like to name, but time and space will not allow me to; however, there are a few that I must openly acknowledge. First, a special thanks to my sistahs of the pen: Audrey Tolliver; Annie Stamps; Airetta Ramey; Lynette O'Neal; Lahn Morris; Eboni Heart; Barbara Thomas; and Cynthia Anglin for their sistah support. A very special thanks is extended to William Mayo and Rose Perkins of Third World Press for providing words of encouragement and invaluable advice. A special thanks to Rose Blouin for introducing me to the works of Zora Neale Hurston at Columbia College.

Thanks to the entire Harrington family, especially my aunts, Eula, Emma and Henrene. Thanks to Taylor Brandy, III; Toni Carter; Tonya Freeman; Linda Ward; Gloria Allen; and Charles Hall for their time and support. Their honest critiques and advice have been a third eye and ear and have helped me a lot. Thanks to Alan Segal, Esq. for his invaluable input. And finally, a special thanks to all of the establishments that have welcomed me to their Open Mic, and to the audiences that enthusiastically cheered me on while reading.

Thanks again.
Nichole L. Shields
October 1997

Preface

The only thing that I can honestly admit to being afraid of is my own success. How often do we shy away from new opportunities by procrastinating until they are no longer there?

Whether we want to face them or not, there are opportunities presented in some form or fashion on a daily basis to many of us, and the easiest way to ignore them is to put our blinders on. This book, just as another one that I am currently working on, has been delayed. The main reason that it is finally in print is the vast number of people who have inquired about it on a daily basis. Yes, for a long time, even with *this* project, I have worn my blinders.

I'm fortunate because I was able to replace with strength and determination the blinders that I wore for so long; for I know that I need both if I want to successfully produce and market my works.

I use the logic that today is too close to tomorrow and tomorrow is not guaranteed, so before another opportunity is presented to us, we must remove our blinders and prepare today for a brighter future.

I hope the above testimony will motivate anyone who may have experienced or is currently experiencing anything that I have just mentioned to remove their blinders and accept the dare that life presents. May the experiences that are presented on the following pages be an eye opener as you wander many roads that I and others have traveled and you, too (perhaps) will have *one less road to travel.*

INTRODUCTION

A part of the poet's responsibility is to explore the inner workings of the heart. Art always means going subsurface to grab meaning from the difficult quarters and callings of the human condition. Poets specialize in the initial deconstruction of their own constitution, heart and soul before they can arrive at an understanding of the music and noise that occupies their culture, family and people.

Writing is a transitional art and poetry is by far its most difficult; it is to language what "jazz" is to music. The inventiveness, internal interrogations, word-dancing and the ability to compact language while keeping it alive, fresh, growing, appealing and saying something is no small order. The best of our poets--and this also applies to fiction and non-fiction writers--age rather quickly because they leave their youthful years in their books as they make their significant statements on paper.

So it is with Nichole Shields in this, her first book. *One Less Road to Travel* is an enduring map of a complicated heart. Her country is not only herself but her community, the streets where she caught buses and trains, where she experienced poverty and belated enlightenment. Ms. Shields is strongest and most sure of herself in the shorter poems, however, it is in her longer works that we glimpse a side of the poet who is evolving and struggling to find and validate her voice. She is as serious as concrete invading unused earth in urban cities. She has a critical eye and is beginning to appropriate a language--her language. She is culturally conscious and her politics do not get in front of her writing as is often the case in first-book poets.

We have to closely watch Ms. Shields. This book is a kick at the door and her entrance confirms her reservation for what is to come.

Haki R. Madhubuti
Poet, Professor of English
Chicago State University

CONTENTS

I often wonder
if people
will like
my poetry

Frankly,
I don't care
From the words
of
Steven Biko
"I Write What I Like"

Southern Hospitality #2

For Arthur and Billie

Not mangos
  kiwis
papayas
pomegranates
Blue or
Rasp
berries

Not Mimosa
Cous Cous
Plantain
Bay or
Afrikan Dew
berries

But Black fathers, brothers, sons,
uncles, and grandfathers

Mothers, yes, mothers too,
as well as sisters, aunts, and daughters

Hanging as loose from the noose
as *Strange Fruit* from its vine.

Freedom

I
like a bird
am free!

I
if I try
can fly
high in the sky

I can build a nest,
leave
and will always know
that it is home

I
like a bird
am free

Because like a bird
I can choose my destination
Spread my wings
and fly away
as the seasons change!

Poison

His first name is Mack
His last name is Daddy
He go ridin' around
in his Black and Silver Caddie

He wears two-toned shoes
with suit and socks to match
he thinks he's God
and the year's #1 catch

His prey are women
both young and old
and when they get out of line
he backhands them with fingers
draped with gold

He carries pockets full of money
far more than anyone that does not work
he thinks he's the shit
but ain't nothin' but a jerk

He hangs around bus depots
and train stations too
looking for troubled run-away girls
because of course
he's got plenty of work for them to do!

Matter of Fact

...............................●
From Nikki Giovanni's
poem entitled 'Nikki-Rosa'

It didn't matter
that we always had
some kind of bread
with our daily one course meals

And if we were lucky,
we were blessed with
some kind of greasy fried meat.

But most importantly,
it didn't matter either that
we never had enuf plates
for everyone and old lard lids
served the purpose just as well
thankyou.

But as Nikki stated,
" ... Black love is Black wealth...
...and all the while, I was quite happy"

and a little hungry too!

Maybe I'll Sell You My Love

You know,
wrapped and presented
like a newborn baby in a soft
smell-good blanket

or
maybe I'll chop, slice,
and dice it up
like the ingredients
for a hot fluffy omelet
Because as we both know,
I tried to give you my love
fair and square,
no strings or requests for
commitments attached --
but you couldn't even
handle that

Yeah, that's what I'll do
Sell you my love
Your 100 percent discount expired.
Yesterday!

Royal Stones

..............................●
Upon the ghastly
discovery of body parts
found on jeffery dahmer's
pantry shelves

Unlawfully removed
were the sacred jewels
more precious than any
ruby or emerald in tiffany's
and larger than any diamond
liz taylor ever saw

Carefully removed
from dahmer's mantel
like award-winning trophies

Mine

The day

the hour

the minute

the second

the first

drop

of

Afrikan Blood

touched American soil,

This country became mine!

The Crack of Dawn

It's not the crack of dawn
when I roll over
open my eyes and see
not the crack of dawn,
but the crack of your ass
slipping into your pants

And I say damn
but am reminded
that you are indeed
another woman's man

And then,
you frown
and I am embarrassed
after I request the impossible,

That you stay
until the crack of dawn.

Rapture

Like the smooth sounds of the
shoo-bee du-wop
bebop music,
your words of love,
  humor and wisdom
hung in the air
caressing my ears
like a once lover
caressed my body

All over and to the soul!

I Said / He Sad

I said: My . is three weeks late

He sad: I'll give you half
                           if you promise to give it
                           back next week -- a car note
                           thing you know

I said: That's OK, I think I have
                           {and I've had} enuf!

He sad: OK, call me if you want.

I: Hung up!

And Another Artist Dies
Known To All Except Her Family

They never understood
why
all the letters came

They never understood
all the telephone calls
and telegrams
and unexpected visits
from people of all walks of life

They never understood
why flowers were sent
from way 'cross the country

They never knew,
They never realized,
that not only did their loved one,
their *strange* loved one,
the one that always wrote
those funny things
on any piece of paper
that she could find

And

they never understood
why she did or said the
things that she did

Again, they just thought
that she was strange!

They never knew,
they never understood,
and perhaps,

they never will.

Just For The Sake of Saying
"I Got A Man"

Even after he sold the TV,
VCR, and Micro-Wave

Sistah girl continued to
put up with the S.O.B.'s
B.S. and his too often case of
V.D.

Just for the sake of saying
"I GOT A MAN"

The Colored Orphan Asylum — NY, 1863

..............................●
After a night of lynching,
castrating and burning
Black men, the cowards
decided to burn Black
children

Sleeping peacefully
throughout
the night, they were
awakened, not by
nature's thunderous
rumbling, but by the roars
of an angry lynch mob,
slurring threats to
"...*burn the nigger's nest...*"

As previously trained for
emergencies, the frightened
children were escorted out the
back door and taken to safe haven

All except for one six-year-old
who found shelter under a bed

Angrily shouting racial slurs while
dashing the orphanage with gasoline,
the mob discovered the little girl...

Brutally beaten,
her body expelled blood
saturating the earth in which she lay
as the blaze stirred like a hungry monster
in the night.

13

Momma in Red

They said
that the only reason
my momma wore a red
dress to her daddy's funeral
was because she hated him
and was just being sassy

I know she wore it
because it was
the only one she had!

Reality

It wasn't because you gained
30 extra pounds after
giving birth to his baby

It wasn't because you lost your job
because you always had to be the
one to take junior to the doctor

It wasn't because looking like a
beauty queen became less important
because you now have a house, husband
and two children to care for daily

It wasn't even because you started
to lose your hair because you worried
more and more --*not because he came
home every night past midnight--*
but because of the unpaid bills and letters
of disconnection that you saw more
than your own reflection in the mirror

Maybe it was because you both had
different agendas fifteen years ago,
and a little more talking out of bed
and fully dressed might have helped!

Trading Places

Classifieds announcing
the arrival of new facades
on old blocks
encouraging all to pack-up
and move to a land
soon to be more promising
than the ads many fell for
decades ago when *dark clouds*
hovered over the *fair city*

With *daylight* approaching
school reform, housing
assistance, and busing will
no longer be needed --
for its inhabitants will be
forgotten in a wasteland called:
The Suburbs!

MADD

His breath
smelled of
flat beer and stale
pretzels

His eyes
were the color
of a hateful bull's
target

The pores of his skin
released more alcohol
than he consumed

His frail body
shook violently

Perhaps he will see
the little boy crossing
the road a mile ahead

Haiku #7

If my tears can wash

away your ignorance, I'll

cry you a river!

Personification

Mystic waters
embracing
roaring winds
while dazzling clouds
caressed the moon
telling it all the beautiful
things it wanted to hear

Ashaki Efuru

..............................●
*African name adopted by
the author on 12/27/95!*

Gracing the Earth
with your presence
while upholding
innocence
in your speech, walk,
and mannerisms

You bring pleasure to all
while spreading love,
peace and happiness
all over theWorld.

Three HairWeave Tips For My "SistahGirlFriends"

TIP #1

Just because the hair is on sale
does not mean that you have
to buy it all, but just in case you
do, please don't wear it all at once.

TIP #2

When wearing the weave, *pleeeaase*
at least use the same color
or as close as possible to
your natural color
TRANSLATION: The white girls
have been complaining that there's
no blond hair left for them.

TIP #3

If your hair was two inches on Friday,
and twenty-five inches on Monday,
Don't make a fool of yourself by
arguing with your co-workers that
Miracle Gro actually works.

..............................●
YES, they lynched
children too!

Darker than a plum
sweeter than a berry
softer than an orange
with a resemblance to
Aunt Mary was the
young ripe fruit that
dangled from the tree!

Haiku #10

Ships sailed carrying

precious human cargo to

unfamiliar lands.

Sweet But Sassy

He tried
to belittle me
before his friends
by saying

YOU GOT BIG LIPS

I said
just as sweet and sassy as a
Louisiana virgin

"How would you know,
you've never been in my panties?!"

Haiku #17 (Lyrics for a Blues Song)

Baby baby oh

Baby you do me much wrong

I just want to die

You Front

*For A.W.
and all the other
revolutionary brothers
that talk Black and sleep
White*

You say that you are a
Black Nationalist and
speak real bad of the
enemy, yet you go home
to his daughter every night

You Front!

You say that you love
being Black and love
Black women because we
are the replenishers of the
world and the most
beautiful creatures on
Earth yet you are loving
Lily-white at night

You Front!

You tell me that I am as
beautiful as Queens
Nzingha, Nefertiti, and
Cleopatra and that I must
continue to breed dark,
strong warriors because
they must be prepared to
fight in the revolution
(when it's time)

Brother,
the revolution will start
right here
right now
just you and me
if you don't get
out of my face with your
b---s---!

Changes

Just before I change your hairstyle
I will enhance your wardrobe,
give you *proper* English lessons,
and enroll you in night classes

All so you can find a better job
and be comfortable around
my friends and family

Haiku #4

You were flattered and

I was embarrassed after

coming on to you!

Haiku #5

The stars and the moon

disappeared into the clouds

the moment you left.

They

In 1595   they called us beasts and savages
as we roamed our native land wearing
royal cloths, cornrows, braids, and 2lb.
diamonds shielded by 24 karat gold
that grew in our backyard.

In 1665   they stole us from our homeland and
forced us, one on top of another, on
top of another, on top of another, in a
3x5 crawl space where we ate, slept,
defecated and often died during the four
plus month journey to the American shores.

In 1785   they inventoried us like chattel, as
they attempted to flog our minds
of any thoughts of home, native
tongue, or rituals.

In 1865   they set us free and we were forced
into yet another form of slavery:
sharecropping!

And now,

In 1995   they told the world that only 450,000
Black people, give or take a few,
were gathered in Washington, DC on
October 16th
But, if we were to listen and believe
their statistics, we would be
exactly what they think we are:
3/5 human!

Haiku #9

In due time, your love

will blossom for me just as

a flower in May!

Young

Leaving the motel, I asked
"...but what if I get pregnant?"

He said,

"Well, we'll just move in
with your mother and
pay her one-hundred
dollars a month for rent!"

Dumb

"We'll go away
for the weekend,
Just you and I"

he promised

Only three weeks
before
he
married
her.

And Full of Come

He often told me
that I'd make someone
a wonderful wife;

Years later, I realized
he never said him.

Haiku #1

Feeling quite aroused

I scream your name in passion

As you enter me!

Haiku #3

Anticipating

Seeing you e-ver-y night

warms my heart and soul.

Fool

Fool,
didn't you know
that we were friends --
best friends?

Did it ever occur to you
that best friends talk and share
secrets while eating from the
same dish of ice cream?

How could you think,
that neither of us
would
ever find out about you
and each of us?

Rent Party

We were some
hip swinging,
lip syncing
finger snapping,
booty shaking
jamming folks at
the party on Friday

The menu consisted of
fried chicken, spaghetti,
coleslaw, potato salad,
ham, and for dessert,
Etta Mae Johnson from
apartment 4D baked 2
homemade apple pies
with chunks of apple
in every bite.

We had a gooood time!

Queen She

With style,
grace, and elegance,
she wears her dreads
with pride,
as cowry shells
dangle from her lobes

She moves through
crowds unnoticed,
and doesn't seem
to mind
while each day
she gives time,
knowledge, and joy
to tender minds
and hope that they will
continue the route in
which she and many
have paved

But,
if they knew half
of her unselfish ways,
she can rest assured that
they will never,
ever,
forget their way home.

Plan C

And on the eighth day,
God said 'let there be Plan,
after Plan, after Plan, after Plan'

Well, it didn't really happen
that way

In fact,
there were blueprints
specifically designed
for each Plan

City blocks of homes
were demolished
and roads were paved
because and for a Plan

Folks arrived in droves
to become a part of the Plan

Family extensions formed
and unity became the norm
as Brothers became keepers,
spreading love, respect and
honor to their women,
all while keeping a watchful
eye on their Plan!

Just Because

Just because
I like to wear my hair cut
short and natural

Just because
I don't have a boyfriend
and don't foresee having
one in the near future

Just because
I am very private and
like to do things by myself

Just because
I have not made passionate
love in a long time

Does not make me a lesbian!

Nerves

With nerves of steel
and a book of complaints
your voice goes unheard
as you complain,
not
to the people that have
"victimized" you
but to the hundreds
of other creatures
that have no regards,
and have never owned
a voter's registration card!

Castrating Women

According to brothas,
'Sistahs don't need
Lorena Bobbitt's knife,
they still have their tongues!'

Truth

White women need
knives
to castrate their men.
Black women need only
to
      write
a book!

Truth of the Matter

Knowledge to the people
all over the land

Once upon a time there
was a woman and a man

Her name was Eve
his name was Adam

Many centuries later
she had the rep of a madam

Some called her cruel
many called her evil

but what folks fail to realize
is that it was Adam's mind
that was feeble

No TKO

Even though
I am big
and tough
with
smooth brown skin
and have the ability
to endure
the many powerful
punches that life
has thrown
in my direction

Does not make
me a punching bag!

After Dinner

I want to wind you like a toy
spin you like a top
and love you and love you
'til your body drop

First, I dance a shimmy
all dressed in black
and with my sweet seductive smile
lure you to my sack

There I'll love you up
and I'll love you down
I'll love you 'til your
head spin 'round and 'round

Then after I'm through
I'll admire you
while you drift off to sleep
the whole night through

Passion

Days
turned
into
nights
and
those
nights
were
transformed
into
mystical
magical
journeys
in
which
we
traveled
the
depths
of
known
and
unknown
familiar
yet
unfamiliar
places
discovering
waterfalls
of
treasures

Happenings

It started
with playful eye rolling
and sweet and sassy sayings

It developed
into an occasional kiss
and a touch and feel
here and there

It transformed into a
stroke of a thigh
and an ever so gentle
caress of the head

And after penetration
things were as they were before

a simple good morning
or good evening
as we passed each other
in the corridor

..............................●

For E.T.
May your tragedy never
be forgotten or repeated

Unforgettable stories,
far from being fairy
told to me as a child,
one in particular
a child
barely in his teens,
accused of reckless
eyeballing;

Days later,
his water filled
body
discovered
Head:
twice its normal size
Body:
with bullet holes and
broken limbs, one
even removed
as cowardly haints
were often
known to do

And for what?

A LITTLE WHITE LIE!

Haiku #13 (Southern Hospitality #5)

Sun shining brightly

on Black bodies hanging like

fruit ready to pick

Haiku #15

Strange species hungry

with greed, stealing and killing

We call them White Folks

Haiku #16 (Remembering Rwanda & Burundi)

Rivers flow of red

innocent blood the Hutus

and Tutsis to blame

Haiku #12 (Us)

The sweet sweaty smell

of lovers passionately

loving all night long

What She Is ...

For Gwendolyn Brooks

..............................●

Griot
Writing
Endless
Notions
Dazzling
Observant
Listeners
Your
Nurturing

Brings
Roots
Out
Of
Kindred
Spirits